2000 Band Names

By David Forbes Brown

2000 BAND NAMES

1. The Usurpers
2. Scabs Unfurled
3. Even We Hate Us
4. Sam I Ain't
5. The Exasperationists
6. Crass Course
7. Trump's Hair to the Throne
8. Men? Oh Pause
9. The Divine Secrets of Yo Yo Ma's Sister
10. Crust
11. Yo We Rump-Roastin'!
12. Give Dong and Prosper
13. The Skin Color Haters
14. Bobafretless
15. Ticking Scone
16. To Be Frank I Am Todd
17. Lady Antivirus
18. Java The Cup
19. Satellite vs. Cable: The Band
20. NostraDamnUs
21. The Passionistas
22. My First Coin

23. Genital Mélange
24. Everyone In This Band Has A Pony
25. Storage!
26. The Representationings
27. We Still Need More of Your Money for Drugs
28. Sexy Hoagie
29. Megadeath Baxter Birney
30. Harmful Yet Swallowed
31. GuberNotorius
32. The Cassettes
33. Us Fellas Curtsy a Lot Is All
34. Rue Barb
35. Kitty Kitty Fang Fang
36. Desk Sex
37. Radon Blast!
38. The Joints of the Chiefs of Staff
39. Bill-Cause-Bye
40. Divagina
41. We Draw a Bath Onstage
42. Glucose Mandate
43. Uruboy And Paraboy Sing
44. The Nasal Sprays
45. Falafel Vortex
46. Row Row Row Your Ass
47. Boring Explosion Clown
48. Fat Wad
49. Keith & John's Urban Legend
50. Lummox
51. The Single Threats
52. Ann Landers: The Band
53. Cattlecall Galactica

266. Small Tree Sex
267. Einstein Burned Breakfast Again
268. The Tappin' Golems
269. Sex With Lasers
270. Buy Our Crap
271. The Department of Transportation Performs
272. Rue More Mills
273. Vagina Bullet
274. Til Blythe Do Us Part
275. Oh Clock!
276. The Inundators
277. Blasphe-Mime
278. Zero Dank Fitty
279. Elephantine Hentzel and The Brioche
280. Wrestling Is the Best Sport
281. Mumps: The Band
282. We Never Use The White Keys On The Keyboard In Our Songwriting
283. We Never Use The Black Keys On The Keyboard In Our Songwriting
284. Fuckaluffaguss
285. The Sixteen Chapels
286. Patton Oswald Pending
287. The Bloody Stools
288. Thanks for the Mammaries
289. Butt-Dial X For Murder
290. Sibling Ribaldry
291. Oats Unencumbered
292. Glacial Hooker
293. The Dharma & Greg Initiative
294. Pepper: Dine

419. The Knot's Not for Naught
420. Breakdancing Bad
421. We Fake Die Onstage & Stay Down
422. Words In Edgewise
423. Gangly & Spanglish
424. For I Am Kaif
425. Sexy Synapse
426. The Walking Keen
427. Holland Tunnel's Opus
428. Yee Haw That's Cornmitment!
429. Ned.I.Am
430. Mega-Choose-Itz
431. Arquette & Larroquette Unplugged
432. 3 Bands Walk Into a Bar
433. Helmet Itch
434. The Infotainment Catacombs
435. Man Date
436. I Can Tell U Ride
437. Gath Blowback & The Trumpeting
     Strumpets
438. Comedy Shrapnel
439. Mormon Moron
440. Commander Riker's Island
441. Matriarch Boy
442. The Attackumentaries
443. Dude That Was Sooo Carl Malden
444. Hick Cup
445. Capos On All Our Basses
446. Gutter Boink
447. Obamas In Pajamas
448. I Am Wont For Want
449. The Bill of Rites of Passage of Bill

450. Constantineantinopal
451. Dramamine Drama Queen
452. We Built This City On Glock-en-spiel
453. Everboy
454. Clem & Time
455. The Wickers of Moisture
456. Jazz Hands Across America
457. Skull Dug-Uppery
458. Nadir Boy
459. A Million Bands To Sunday
460. The Drapes
461. Yo We Displaced Like Water in a Cylinder
462. Platypi
463. In Me Flat
464. The Catsup on the Rye
465. Missile Crotch
466. I Did Not Inhale With That Woman
467. Heterogloben
468. Paper-Machet Gary and his Pellet-Hiding Low-Riders
469. Lectern Doctrine
470. The Undulators
471. Our Secret Ingredient Is Hate
472. Cops On Llamas
473. Full Chortle
474. Where the Sun Don't Shine
475. This Band Will Live In F-n'-G
476. Night Cow
477. Andy's And Dee's
478. The Nailgunned Tongues
479. Sexy Cockroach

480. Captain, We Have Engaged The Blog
481. SubterFugue
482. Dentures, Depends and Gerry
483. The Rued
484. Totes Adorbs!
485. Sack O' Fingers
486. Reach Out & Fuck Someone
487. Horton Heard a Herd
488. The Circumcisers
489. Here We Go Round the Store-Bought Waffles
490. Discomrobertulated
491. Paypal: The Band
492. The "3's-a-Crowd" Eleven
493. If Not For the Grace of Lenny
494. Chunk
495. A Comedy of Lasers
496. Yo We Cornfed Yo
497. Tethered to a Douche
498. Play Kate
499. The Shuntaholics
500. Abbadabadboy
501. Shunt Me a Dream
502. Lord of the Sass
503. The Potatoes
504. Hotsex Moe and The Slippery Triplets
505. Our Bad
506. Fennel, Is All
507. To Curtail Or Not To Curtail
508. TagliaD'oh!
509. Centriflugelhorn Force
510. Tender Bumpkin

511. The "Then a Sensible Dinner"s
512. Angry Boy & Bitchy Gal
513. Toot In Common
514. Orphan is the New Black
515. Metal Acuity
516. The Voices In Our Heads Sing Better
517. Fundemic!
518. Honor LuLu
519. For Fifty Amber Waves of Gray
520. As You Were
521. There Was a Band From Nantucket
522. The Pre-Owned Vehicles
523. Totes Insignif
524. Upstairs Larry
525. Dandy Lion
526. If Only You'd Let Us Do More For You
527. Unacceptaboy
528. Tepid Blitzkrieg
529. The Grand Poo Bear
530. Slowly I Toined
531. Parenthetical Dungarees
532. Mostly Just Ramparts
533. Fun w/ Al Bundy at the Bay Of Fundy
534. Pollywannanomial
535. The Misanthropening
536. Draw Us a Bath
537. Bless Me Father For I Have Killed
538. Night of a Couple Stars
539. Sack O' Bats
540. The Other White Keys
541. "Trendy" Boy & "With-It" Gal!
542. Bona Vibe

543. Fuck Ewe
544. Everyone In This Band Is Named Horace
545. Mouth To Ass
546. He Walks Like a Lady
547. The Hotsexy President Nixons
548. We Put the Drama In Dramamine
549. Slap Trunk
550. Bad Mitten
551. Jack The Rapper
552. The Sousaphone-It-Ins
553. Your Tax $ Funds Us!
554. DJ Yo Yo Is Black In Session
555. Ya Jamoke Ya
556. Pear-Shaped Danny Partridge in a Pear Tree
557. Nincompoopapalooza
558. A Myriad of Plethoras
559. For Pork You Pine
560. The Greta Van Susterens
561. We Built This City On Polka & Lies
562. Ab-BRO Cadab-BRAH
563. Excretion Discretion
564. Bubba Gump & The Sump Pumps
565. On Golden Blond
566. Totes Bourgeois
567. That Golem's Made From Woodstock Mud!
568. Shempnado
569. The Majestic Pantheon Of Whatevs
570. Under the Dork
571. Lullaboy The Crooner Boy

603. Faceboocket Challenge
604. Onslut
605. Forensic Penis
606. The Bequeathers
607. "Scratch-Ticket" Gupp & The Plasmatronics
608. We Best Pee First
609. Your Inheri-Lance
610. Funageddon!
611. The Purloined Laser
612. Scuzzy Wuzza Wuzza Scuzz
613. Handblown
614. Metal Clarity
615. He Left His Slip In Islip
616. John Rats In Burger
617. The Deviated Septums
618. We're Your 12th Cousins Thrice Removed!
619. Tugboy
620. Plasticine Vagina
621. Rock-a-Fella
622. The Idiomatic Idiots in the Attic
623. Ned Vader: Dark Side Plumbing
624. Heck & The Handcart
625. Our Narcissism Runneth Over
626. The Sexaphones
627. Doug Llewelyn's Hair
628. The Price of Gas Lately
629. Apple Brown Hussy
630. Socialites On The Make
631. The Individual Proton Whisperer

661. $: Our Daily Bread
662. The Bundle Of Sticks
663. O' The Ilk
664. Sodium-Chlorinatrix Peppers Ya With Song
665. Intangiboy
666. Klandestine Kowards Kill
667. Sprechen Sie *Douche*
668. Olive Branch of the Military
669. Inject Shun
670. We Are Everydork
671. Griddle-Cake Moe and his Connie Povich Nineteen
672. Rectumify
673. The Plastic Dispensers
674. Brokedick Mountain
675. Dullards With Crullers
676. A Murder of Crows and Mimes
677. David BONEanaz – Get It?!
678. The Definite Maybes
679. Cremora Ice Cream
680. Release The Dongs
681. Pancake-Makeup Grizelda & The Trowels
682. Disney's "Malwarefficient"
683. Damn Nation
684. JP Power & Assholeiates
685. Yo Trippin' Balls Duh Yo
686. Mr. Lady Boy
687. Manic Mundane
688. The Undeserving Doted Upon
689. Lorenzo's Llamas

777. Puppy Ciao
778. Circa 19-Whatevs, Brah
779. Carol Channing On The Outer Hull Captain
780. Ahh That's The Spot
781. Peoter's Plastic Happy Place
782. We Plum Ain't Good
783. Another War Between CGI and Humans
784. Groundup
785. 1313 Munster Lightning
786. Monkey See, Jared Do
787. Boy Meets Jo Anne Worley
788. Puppy Soup
789. Manny Ramirez Lip Snycs To Crap
790. The Shoe Must Go On
791. Urinator III: The Final Squirt
792. Stench Mount
793. Geoparty Jeopardy
794. Ten Spun Moments with Tab
795. Ocupado
796. We're Also a Notary!
797. Ho Broken
798. The Deathasizers
799. Hunk 'A Steamin' Crunk
800. Jar Jar Fetch Massa's Shoes
801. Clownado
802. Fupa Faux Pas
803. Telly SaveAllOfUs & The Lollies
804. Runny
805. For The Love Of Ned
806. Bio Evanescence

807. The Heterosexers
808. Talkin' Down At Ya
809. The N-Words!
810. Ordinance: The Band
811. Barbara Walter's "Sex Thump" Tour
812. The Ghost OF Mrs. Muir
813. We're Better As An App
814. The Bedfellows
815. Blitzed Craig
816. Sexin' the Hubs
817. Totes Butch
818. Mast O' Don
819. Catacomb Clown
820. The Mammonaters
821. Slipdork
822. Fryolatrix and her Whip-Oils
823. Free Gaffer Tape!
824. Tale Spin
825. All Zhuzhed-Up
826. I Suck
827. Party Flavors
828. The Widow McGarnagle
829. Justickleyoulate
830. Bob Saget & The Temple of Doom
831. Podium Mime
832. The Sleestaks Three
833. Alfred, Lord Teddy's Son
834. Bitch Itch
835. Thank You For Letting Us Love You
836. Just Recantin'
837. The Smasher in the Eye
838. Pork Chops & Applesauce: The Band

839. Sumner Summers and The Fall
840. If Only We Mated
841. The Streets Of San Jacinto
842. Talk To Me In Foreign Tones Linda
843. The 3-Note Melodies
844. Nuttin' But Millet
845. We Pretend to Crucify People On
     Stage!
846. The Eveningers
847. Yo 5-'n & Dime-'n It Yo
848. Stormtroopin' With Blanche
849. Drained Trannie
850. The "Juxta" Posers
851. We Do Our Taxes Onstage
852. PR Nightmare
853. Baby... I'm the Greatest
854. The Cum Loudly's
855. Stoked & Mounting
856. Your Credit Card
857. Don't Tell My Wife We're Here
858. The Impenetrables
859. Clodhoppy: The Dorky Bunny
860. Secular Prayer
861. Gutterboy
862. We Rent Our Sackcloths On Stage!
863. Mausoleum Mime
864. Hunkerin' Wit' Chunky-D
865. The Wettening
866. Bedonkadoctor
867. Shep Will Allow It
868. Kerfuffle Nation
869. EGOTs For All!

870. Much Prancing About
871. The Mildly Perturbed
872. Haberdasherboy
873. Johnny 2-Kyles & The Mordant Splendor
874. We Say Friggin' Insteada Fuckin'
875. Jehovah Fat
876. Just a Light Show
877. The Potato Boat Quotient
878. A Trace Of Atkins Was Found
879. With Bells On
880. Parenthetical Abyss
881. Dungaree-Boy & Skort-Gal
882. The Rot
883. Captain Happenstance
884. MYlennial!
885. Hot Is Cleveland From Family Guy
886. Mimes In REAL Cages
887. See Men
888. The Overly-Priced Items
889. Golly Gee Knome
890. Umpteen Teen Umps
891. Sacrostank
892. Don Ricklesbaum & The Matzo Balls
893. Pasture Eyes
894. The Fallow Fellows
895. Yo We Purloined
896. Stouffer's Welsh Rarebit Presents
897. Butterboy
898. Own My Worst Enemy
899. Mommy Deer Rest

900. Might As Well Face It You're a DICK Ted
901. The Stacked Decks
902. Cous Cous Achoo
903. Nuttin' But Lanyards
904. Sticky Boy & Gummy Gal
905. The Injectionaters
906. Fox Burrow
907. Everybody Tolerates Cludmond
908. Moon Bloodkeen
909. Kill To My Loo
910. Our Look of Fine Lines
911. The Burnished
912. Ancient Mime Burial Grounds
913. Sex With Haggis
914. Pop & Lock & Load
915. Next, on "The Left Wing"
916. Scat
917. The Aggressive Short-Hair Chicks
918. Release the Crack
919. Self-Depracatin' Sum-Bitches
920. Whip It Keen
921. A Mic Mac's Tic Tac
922. Extra Extra Care All About It!
923. Borsht Bundt
924. Me Scalp-um White Man Ticket
925. The Closet Organizers
926. Sergeant Schultz's Luftwaffles
927. VIAGRA: The Band
928. Kyle In The Hole
929. Hulk Smash Lottery Ticket
930. Mottled Boy

931. The Write-Offs
932. All Our Amps Are On the Clapper
933. Dour Dork
934. Yo Yo Putta Needle Onna Rekud
935. Spinsters On Tour
936. Pompadourk
937. Death By Fabric Softener Bear
938. Brake Spring
939. I Thee Pretend
940. Dicky Conceiver & The Chromosomes
941. Rabies In Accounting
942. The Nowadays Gals
943. Puny Beads Everywhere!
944. Estimated Hex
945. Trending Lumpington
946. The Newborn Puppies of Satan
947. Pink Slime Soufflé
948. Molester Mister
949. Tannin Bomb
950. Whisper To Me In Your Low Register
     Linda
951. Agog
952. The Totem Insects
953. Richard In A Box
954. New Bile
955. Infrafracture
956. The Squirtables
957. Blythe Begat Kyle Begat Leif Begat
     Blyle
958. Kimoto Drag Queen
959. Thumb Squat
960. Death Boy & Disease Gal!

961. The Clumping Agents
962. Placid Master
963. L'il Dumber Boy
964. Sexy Dentistry
965. Johnny Blasphemy Toots His Own Thang
966. Sure Burt
967. The Walking Dumb
968. Mavis Get The Phone
969. BTW - WTF
970. We Is Ironical An' Like 'Dat
971. Smuckers: The Band
972. The Caterwauls
973. Burgled Meat
974. Kyle Shall Remain Nameless
975. Utility Nun
976. Unbelievaboy
977. The Dust Mite Whisperers
978. Kick Smarter
979. Rock Hard (Yes We Mean THAT)
980. Mr. Sister
981. That Cruller Is Moving On Its Own!
982. Gig Reflex
983. Fonzie & Potsie's Scheme
984. Trenchgina
985. Crapshoot Wisdom
986. The Gizzards
987. The Artist Not Formerly Known
988. Our Hour
989. Skull Tongue
990. Bag-'Em Tag-'Em Taggert The Braggart

991. Stench Splotch
992. The Awfully Wed
993. Expungo The Clown
994. Fair Moans
995. See Us For What We Aren't
996. The Jogging Dead
997. Trickle-Down Clearly Works
998. Norma & Norman Ain't Normal
999. VendeTA-DA!
1000. We Find the Defendant... Sexy
1001. Mumps & Sons
1002. Cloudy With a Chance of Mimes
1003. That's What Me Said
1004. Peek-A-Boy Sings 'N Hides
1005. The Bubble-Heads
1006. Click Tick Clack Tock
1007. Perp Pie
1008. Aquaduct Sclumberblatch Sings
1009. The Receiving End
1010. We Throw Pillows!
1011. Illegitimate Grampa
1012. Yo Yo Pop The Drop
1013. The Homofeeliacs
1014. Tell Me How To Cry Linda
1015. The Hearty Nancy Boys
1016. Clean 'Em & Line 'Em Up
1017. The Orgy Brothers
1018. Wavy in the Navy as Davy Spills Gravy
1019. Unisexy
1020. We're 100 If We're a Day
1021. Orifice Mime

1053. Ceremonial Clown
1054. The Archetypical Swaths Of Lenny
1055. Sugared Laser
1056. Everbone
1057. Mylar Platform
1058. Cuff Me, Boys
1059. Mayor Rob Ford's Hot Pipe Roundup
1060. The Ginsu Knives
1061. Clearasil: The Band
1062. Jimmy Fallon's Truck
1063. Scabies On Toast
1064. Rutting Douche
1065. The Culpabilities
1066. Alotta Pointing
1067. Daft Drunk
1068. Fred Rogers & Satan's School For Sluts
1069. Snoredom
1070. Autopsy Mime
1071. The Vouchers
1072. Meteoric Crash
1073. Florence, Blythe 'n Gail
1074. Gray's Sports Anatomy
1075. Blaspha-Me!
1076. The Ginger & Lou Grants
1077. Under The Known
1078. How'd Ya Like a Bucket 'a Ned?
1079. Tumult
1080. Some Like It Haysbert
1081. The Fine Family of Family-Like Corporations
1082. Constant Teen

1083. Ant Man Cries Uncle
1084. Turn A Kit
1085. The "Not That There's Anything Wrong With That" Tour
1086. Jizzmattaz!
1087. Ass Backwards
1088. Pampered Bastard
1089. Listen To Bitchy-Poo Y'all!
1090. The Hectares
1091. Perp Fiction
1092. "Only Our Left Hemispheres" Perform
1093. Earl's A Girl!
1094. The Butterball Warblers
1095. We Is Seminole An' Like 'Dat
1096. Hugh Manatee
1097. Engorgement
1098. Commemorating Products
1099. St. Elmo's Lighter
1100. The Band Names Oh Ha Ha
1101. Yo Yo Megabelle Swingin' It
1102. Just Haunches
1103. Peoter Hides Hot Dogs While Performing
1104. Bless Me Father For I Have Sneezed
1105. Circumferencization
1106. Forbidden Stretch
1107. That Dog From The Grinch
1108. Mimes In Mud
1109. Cankle Party
1110. Dissertation Bieber
1111. The Equidistant

1112. Two Dorks, an Ass and a Pizza Place
1113. Yooztopia
1114. Blyle & The Blow-Pops
1115. Vapid Skank
1116. Culled From Braggarts
1117. The Power Of Leif
1118. Grassy Ass
1119. Disgust Musk
1120. Wilma Flintstone & The Family Stone
1121. Sacroshemp
1122. The Rehearsal Spaces
1123. Thaddeus Thoates Thwarts Thrice
1124. Fiber!
1125. Monkey Clause
1126. Explosion at the Doily Plant
1127. Dumpster Mime
1128. Giving Up Lent Ha Ha
1129. The Margaret Thatchers
1130. Country Crock: Of Shit
1131. Quid Pro D'oh!
1132. Valhalla Eviction Notice
1133. Hey Peaches And/Or Freckles
1134. Talisman About Town
1135. Urkel & The Family Stone
1136. We're All Pregnant!
1137. The Bogarting
1138. Fabric Softener Bear Sex
1139. Glen Kyle Glen Blythe
1140. Level Rebel
1141. Palm Her "Anian"
1142. Sulu's Solo

1171. Dewey Decimal System: The Band
1172. Reminiscense
1173. Tactile Oblivion
1174. The Whore-able
1175. Rod & His Staff Comfort You
1176. Hit Ya Mark Ya Bastard
1177. Rank Blanket
1178. I Con
1179. We Never Go To The 5th!
1180. The Pratfallen
1181. Dolly Parting & The Red Seas
1182. Peel Back Our Flaky Layers
1183. Tendergroin
1184. The Damp Squadron
1185. Yo He a Cheesy Cracker
1186. Rubba Dub Dubya
1187. Book Grope
1188. Lady-O Goo-Goo
1189. The Merman Diaries
1190. Stank Dance
1191. Eye Of Newt Blood Of Mime
1192. Chachi In Charge
1193. We Hand Out Black Goth Tortilla Chips!
1194. Metrosensual
1195. Who Ain't Love L'il Fucklet?
1196. The Rehearsals
1197. Erudite Scumbag
1198. Bargain Garbage
1199. Mystery On Rizzoli Isle
1200. The Youths Hostile
1201. Mally: The Rally Mallard!

1202. Indubitaboy
1203. Cursive Expletive
1204. Burgess Megadeath
1205. Little Red "Ride Me" Ho (In the Hood)
1206. Belieber You Me
1207. The Burping Tubs
1208. Dorks Du Jour
1209. With Ma Gal It's Magotes!
1210. Snug As Doug Wearing A Rug
1211. Hypocrischristy
1212. Public Enemy No. One-Billion
1213. Military Mime
1214. The Kristy McNichols
1215. Put Us Over Your Knee
1216. Just Statistics!
1217. Trilobite Sandwich
1218. Repeating the Chorus Yet Again
1219. The Two Doors
1220. Josie and the Pussy
1221. Did We Turn The Oven Off?!
1222. The Big Easy She Be
1223. J'accuse!
1224. Jack Klugman On Your Trellis With Roses
1225. Xanadon't
1226. "The Man" Performs
1227. Streaming Mimi
1228. Five Kazoos & The Truth
1229. The On-Call-agists
1230. Rectum Requiem
1231. Tanta-Liza!

1232. Dulcimer Implosion
1233. Plastics Make Ned Possible
1234. We Wish We Were Down Your Pants
1235. Clamor
1236. The Yawn Birds
1237. Preening With Weezy
1238. Now With Only 1-5 In The Bass!
1239. Hippie Storm
1240. The Gorton Fisherman "Sex-Thrusts"
1241. Mostly Donny Most
1242. Oil 'A Broilin'
1243. We See Bored People
1244. Wha Choo Talkin' 'Bout Mr. Drummin'?!
1245. Gourmand Mime
1246. Do the Math
1247. The Heavy Petters
1248. Moon Over Sheboygan
1249. Suzie's All A-Strut
1250. Glass Cow
1251. Slippery Periodical
1252. The Ghost Of Tony The Tiger
1253. Captain Sass
1254. Shake, Rattle & Droll
1255. We Have Too Much Twine!
1256. The Flaming Pips
1257. Starlet Harlot
1258. Chris Christie's "Bridge To Success" Tour
1259. ExcreMental
1260. The Babes Butch

1261. Marmot Shunt
1262. Abe Vigoda & The Sex-Squats
1263. Cracker Stank
1264. Asplundh: The Band
1265. The Most Dampest Moist-Men
1266. Carny Art By Art Carney
1267. Totes Elongated
1268. Eating Nemo
1269. Preliminary Bullocks
1270. The "OJ Is Clearly Innocent" Neptet
1271. Grab Hag
1272. The Ruts
1273. Where But By The Grace Of Ned
1274. Holy Water Sno-Cone
1275. We Just Wanna Watch Our Stories
1276. Do The Dirt-Bag Rag
1277. Fedexerer
1278. Prague Rock
1279. Nip/Tuck/Sneeze
1280. The Martin-Short-As-Carl-Sagans
1281. Endocrine Stew
1282. Musical Spam
1283. No Motor Cars
1284. Chip Chocolates & his Off The Ol'
       Block Chaps
1285. The Fuckaneers
1286. Gamey Vegan
1287. Yo Yo Rip Torn & Rip Taylor F-in' *Rip
       It Yo*
1288. Boygatory
1289. Irreverent Sot
1290. The Excommunicatin'

1291. Lights, Camera, Cletus!
1292. Sex Bucket
1293. Roker Roker Roker Your Boat
1294. Thang Snap
1295. We Use The Word "Eatery"
1296. The Desiccants
1297. Shellackin' With The Gooch
1298. Oh It's Monday Oh Ha Ha
1299. Sexy Habit (Nun Version)
1300. Balki Bartakalypse
1301. Saved By The Bowl
1302. Mimes.gov
1303. Only-One-Chord Verses!
1304. We Also Deal Drugs
1305. A-Rod's Delicate Poetry Cakes
1306. The Monikered
1307. Bang Thang
1308. Tommy Johnnyhawk & The Bolted Screws
1309. Floozy Palooza
1310. The Sexperiments
1311. Is Roy Al
1312. Birth Control In Twizzler Form
1313. Herman Munster & The Family Stone
1314. Too Much Scaffolding
1315. Placating Bathbort
1316. The Swallowing Trollops
1317. Scientellmeallaboutit!
1318. I Am Keif – Yes, "Keif"
1319. Get Out Of Care Free Card
1320. The Brassholes

1350. Wynona Ride Her
1351. Tapir Burgers For All!
1352. Dour Hour
1353. The Comedy Rosetta Stones
1354. Lady Boy
1355. Driving Miss Weezy
1356. My Kingdom for a Nosegay
1357. Working Late in the Orifice
1358. Mimes Chewing Tobacco
1359. Grady From Sanford & Son Gotz
      Himz Pantz Onna Groun'
1360. Scootch!
1361. Damsels In Express
1362. Untrue That
1363. The Dukes of Hasselhoff
1364. Weeblo Me
1365. Blow On Our Soup
1366. Sit And Ubu Sat
1367. Hold For Editing
1368. "Declotay" Larry and The Endless
      Little Cakes
1369. Zany Crypt
1370. The Proclivities
1371. Oh Yoooooou!
1372. The Ladies of The View Sing
      Different Songs Simultaneously
1373. Mimenado
1374. Sunny & Share
1375. What Parts Of Who Are In These
      Hefty Bags
1376. Mix Up at the Comedy Nursery
1377. Sketchy Idget

1405. Muddy Bagel
1406. Ol' Jed's Under That Golly-Darn Ol' Lookin' Glass
1407. Emineminate
1408. The Mormon TaberNyquil Choir
1409. Hoof In Mouth
1410. Iron Boy and The Starter Capes
1411. Taxidermy On Humans
1412. The Boring Mission Statements
1413. Indigenous Mime
1414. Clyde & Dale's Clydesdales
1415. Rum In Spring Ahhh
1416. Let's Go Metric Anyway!
1417. Crockett In The Tub
1418. The Rife
1419. Ozone Playa
1420. Betty White and The Klingon Birds Of Prey
1421. Two Dudes Diverged In Wood
1422. The Squataholics
1423. Tell Me I'm Pretty, Officer
1424. Urkel Twerks
1425. Broken Back From Mounting
1426. David, Let Her, Man
1427. Ma Tricked You Late
1428. Hold Me Closer Boring Stanza
1429. The Pincers
1430. Temperance & Sealy Are Our Actual Names
1431. Pie Holes Engage
1432. Tickle My "Elmo"
1433. The Greenest Grass Is On Our Side

1434. "Stanky-Rank" Hank Tanks
1435. Escape to Which Mountain?
1436. Copping An Aptitude
1437. The Gurgling Tummies
1438. Slutty Or Talented—You Decide
1439. Johnny Woocares and The Tertiary Blame-Engine
1440. Bobbing For Aplomb
1441. Ego Killed Our Depth
1442. The Colloquialisms
1443. For I Am Torg Of Housewares
1444. His-Bowl-Ya
1445. To Quaff Or Not To Quaff
1446. Take The Nestea Suicide Plunge
1447. The Openly Gay Cops
1448. Progressive's Flo with Rush
1449. Duck!
1450. We Think Slavery Is Bad
1451. Of Utmost Impotence
1452. The UnintentIONAL CAPS
1453. Pantaloon Platoon
1454. He's a Poet Laureate & Doesn't Know It, Gloria
1455. Gluten For All!
1456. Clowns In Sewage
1457. Donner Party Of One
1458. The Roiling Broils
1459. Taze Me Henrietta
1460. Wood That We Could
1461. Cattle Gal & The Mandibulas
1462. Late To The Party
1463. Beauty and the Douche

1464. Fallow Playa
1465. Wax-Yet-Robots of Nixon & Hendrix
      Perform
1466. Ring My Dong
1467. The Gerber Baby Raps
1468. Hither And/Or Yon
1469. Shempcompoop
1470. You're Our Appendage!
1471. I Norman Fell For You
1472. Catholic Gold & The Starving
      Children
1473. Structured Crap
1474. The VHS Videocassettes
1475. Pre Mortem
1476. Delusion Contusion
1477. We Make Toast Onstage
1478. Gumption Junction
1479. The Untalented Critics
1480. Gut Suck
1481. I Now Pronounce You Douchebag &
      Ass-Bitch
1482. Pratfall Platform
1483. We Take No For An Answer
1484. Joey Dumplings and The Electric
      Lunchpails
1485. Fake Happy!
1486. The Rumored Only-Okay
1487. Thorax Soufflé
1488. Hurricane Shecky
1489. Skanktown Races Sing Sang Sung
1490. Inaugural Twerk
1491. The Bated Breaths

1492. Ralph Mouth Hits His Mark
1493. Mr. Bland-Man Bring Me a Dream
1494. I Thee Love, Buddy
1495. The Digestible Chunks
1496. Knock Knock—We're There!
1497. Dour Milieu
1498. The Fellow Enthusiasts
1499. Chortle
1500. So Re, Do Mi a Fa (vor brah) and
      Fetch Mi a La Ti
1501. Bandied About
1502. The Myriad Vortices o' Helene
1503. Trail-Blazing Into Boredom
1504. Ancillary Chutzpah
1505. Paper-Pushing Lard-Ass Klingon
1506. Yo We Bonks
1507. Upstairs Larry's Listening
1508. A Day That Will Live In Infinity
1509. Fiberglass & Gum
1510. The Dissertatin' Hillbillies
1511. Kyle-On-Kyle Action
1512. Bitch In Heels On Wheels For Reals
1513. Sound Clumps
1514. Been There Fun That
1515. No Direction
1516. Drag Us Clicking and Screaming To
      Your Desktop
1517. The Contiguous Band
1518. Mongo Conduct Orchestra Now
1519. Telltale Dickey
1520. Born & Raised In Scheneckticazoink
1521. Gall Bladders In Sauce

1550. Rabies, Scabies & Davie
1551. For All: In Tents With Purposes
1552. The Boobs
1553. It's OK I'm With the Band
1554. Felicity's Facetious Fetish-Fest
1555. Papa Maou Maou
1556. Rabies & Cinnamon Stick
1557. I Was a Pip
1558. Debilitatrix and her Squadron of
     Moes
1559. Rehoboth Row Boat
1560. Manscaping With Jorge
1561. Jelly Do Not
1562. We Sport Different Handbags Every
     Song!
1563. The Gooseflesh
1564. Cyborg Nun
1565. Barely Discernible Grunts and a
     Triangle
1566. Circle Twerk
1567. The Marketing Techniques
1568. Urine Submarine
1569. Those 3 Monkeys With the Eyes
     Ears Mouth Thing
1570. Blubberdashery
1571. Feel Our Boring Pain
1572. Mayor McJizz & The Yes Men
1573. Garage Mirage
1574. Totes & Toodles!
1575. Mock 10 Merry Go Round
1576. The Erudite Hookers
1577. Toby McWhyagonandunnit

1578. Memory: The Boring Form of Intelligence
1579. Interactive Hoagie
1580. Water Me Like the Plants Herbert
1581. Equinox Mime
1582. What McSteamy May Come
1583. Always All Ways
1584. If You Applaud Too Loud We'll Give You a Time Out
1585. The Puniest Pastry Puffs
1586. Hey There Jorge Boy
1587. Not How It's Done
1588. Little Miss Gofuckabison
1589. Smelling Old GI Joes
1590. Hot in Zimbabwe
1591. Lurch from The Addams Family and The Family Stone
1592. Me So Horn Section-y
1593. Nubile Hussy
1594. The Gooch's Pocket Comb
1595. Way-Gay Pitter-Patter
1596. Shields, Yarnell and Oates
1597. We're Always Eating When We Talk
1598. Only Whistles!
1599. Mimetic Bramble
1600. Ancient Tween Wisdom
1601. This Space For Rent
1602. Tony McMeltingclocks and Dawn
1603. Notary Dame
1604. Claymore Trip Wire Sex
1605. That Kool Aid Guy/Thing With a Recorder

1606. Live Keen Or Die
1607. The Star Trek Basements
1608. Deciduous Rapture
1609. Sing To My Stomach Moonzelda
1610. Comp Our Meals
1611. American False Idol
1612. Treat Williams Well My Son
1613. Sewer Clown University
1614. Toned Down For You Sensitive Folk
1615. Gad's Morbid Historium
1616. Trap Door Sex
1617. Get On the Molly Trolly Kids!
1618. US Postal Tramp Stamps
1619. Well Ain't That a Swift Kick in the Jowels
1620. Dirge Binge
1621. Crotch Igniter
1622. The Lord's Name in Vain Like a Hundred Times
1623. Megadeath Vieira
1624. We're Snorting Coke While You Wait
1625. Earwax & Wicks
1626. "L'il Bashfull" Explodes In Song
1627. The Extremely Fake Lightsabers
1628. Sit On My Lap Ya Goose
1629. Clifford's Boring Labyrinth
1630. God's Plant Landed Us in Satan's Jail
1631. Modern Medicide
1632. The In-'n-Out Sexburgers
1633. For Lorne
1634. These Are My Favorite Notes!

1635. Do the Oligarchy Strut
1636. Give Biodiversitron Your Earth Women
1637. Biff's Honkin' Schnoz
1638. Zeitgeist Lexicon
1639. Sang Thang
1640. Wedded Bitch
1641. The Granules
1642. Get Lena on the Horn
1643. It's Not That We Totally Suck
1644. Chemical Sandwich
1645. Sexy Pope Sex
1646. Dicky Tuxedo & The Cumberboys
1647. The Guppies
1648. Enamored 'Cuz Hammered
1649. Monsoon To Be
1650. Track Marks & Clarified Butter
1651. What Mites Have Been
1652. Adelaide's Goat Gotten
1653. The Bastion Of Citadels
1654. We Store Our Bucket Lists in Actual Buckets
1655. Holding Courtney
1656. Puninterest
1657. Fornication Matrix
1658. Logan's Run: The Disco Tour
1659. Sketchy Ottoman
1660. Blubber Band
1661. The Countess Conundrum
1662. Shooting Blanks
1663. To and Afro

1664. That Guy Who Played Canon Reanimated
1665. Meat Trowel
1666. Analweiss
1667. Remembering Zortron
1668. Twerk the Night Orgasmic
1669. Yougogurt
1670. Two Disco Trains Diverged In a Wood
1671. The Sex
1672. Varicose Weather
1673. For I Am Talis Man
1674. Amish Synchronous Orbit
1675. Yo Yo Playa Duh Yo
1676. Joni Finally Divorces Chachi
1677. Check Out Our Cocky Gate!
1678. Tantrum Anthem
1679. Crabapple Cove Lane, Newark
1680. Lyle Waggoner: Now In Color!
1681. Cake Rifle
1682. The Yoozniverse
1683. Wreaking Halibut
1684. Cleaning Carl Sagan's Bong
1685. Vixen Compote
1686. Reeking of Havoc
1687. Mavis Get Me a Beer
1688. The Umbilical Chords
1689. Our Agent Says Hi
1690. Fruitford Has Sex With Assorted Fruits On Stage
1691. Cymbalism
1692. The Sucklings

1749. Curse Correction
1750. Eunice and/or Mavis Performs
1751. Death By Coin Collection
1752. Animal Husband
1753. Those Plastic Tips on the Ends of Shoelaces
1754. We Only Do Assemblies
1755. Erecting Lenny
1756. We Break Up Onstage Every Gig
1757. Myopic Succulence
1758. The Mr. Drummonds
1759. **God Kills Those Who Disagree With God**
1760. Buckle & Rupture
1761. Dope o' Mine
1762. Only One Chord!
1763. OK Class Take Out Your Klingon Language Workbooks
1764. Cat Skills
1765. Load-Bearing Wheat Roll
1766. Drag Me To Your Desktop, Gunter
1767. Pet Mosquito
1768. Tin Roof... Fixed and Painted!
1769. The Rolling Rosetta Stones
1770. Stuff You, You Turkey
1771. Clownhenge
1772. Robert Urich: Discuss
1773. Chimney Sex
1774. Pachelbel's Canon of Massive Death
1775. **SmashRalphMouth**
1776. Dick-In-Pie Productions Presents
1777. Scary Masks Make Us "Interesting"

1778. Abe Vigoda and The Family Stone
1779. The Cramps
1780. Mongo Sing and Smash Guitar
1781. You Got Soap On My Scone
1782. Pelosibot Reboot
1783. We All Fake Die On Stage And Stay Down
1784. This Is Our Band Name
1785. Time Daily
1786. Your Thang Is In My Peanut Butter!
1787. The Bobby Bradys
1788. Knock-Knockin' At You Do-oooooo
1789. Muddy Cruller
1790. Hot & Oily Robot Sex
1791. Rory from The Gilmore Girls Raps
1792. The Wedgies
1793. Boring Bravado
1794. Sea Bisquit and The Peanut-Butter Mouth-Roofs
1795. For Those About To Suck
1796. The Fitty-Percent Offs
1797. Peoter's Pee Odor
1798. Now With Heterosexuality!
1799. The Jack Klugman Experience
1800. We Are Latex Scup Bucket
1801. It's Sleeting Men
1802. Tattoo From Fantasy Island "Shatners" Some Ditties
1803. Thunderclown
1804. The Spiro Agnews
1805. *Blood Storm* - Ooooo!
1806. Totem Brown Guy

1807. Ain't Shart On My Dreams Brah
1808. The Mosquito Whisperers
1809. Hold Me Mr. Putin
1810. Stench Attempt
1811. The Evil Rascals: Starring Spelunky and Al Falafel
1812. 5 Hours of Baseball Organ Music!
1813. Titilatrix and her Edible Outerwear
1814. Tugboat Galactica
1815. Flock of Hair-Gells
1816. Carlton The Doorman Sings From Behind the Curtain
1817. Selfish Crying
1818. Carbs... Am I Right People?
1819. It Takes 2 to Tae Bo
1820. The Counter-Indicated
1821. A Very Brady Orgy
1822. Shake Rattle and Who Gives a Shit
1823. Klinger on the Runway
1824. Glue Guns & Tap
1825. That Thing's Head Is On That Stick
1826. Montessouri: The Band
1827. We Forget Who Declan Cannon Is
1828. Outhouse Flower
1829. Snakes in the Bass Drum!
1830. Tyrone and Tyrell Do The Rap
1831. Irony: The Band
1832. Staff Confections
1833. Kittens in the Bass Drum!
1834. For I Am Foam Trance
1835. The Only-Slightly-Humorous Commercials

1836. Sod of Mites
1837. Free Papsmears Backstage
1838. Everybody Connie Chung Tonight
1839. Not Us, Just Swamp Gas
1840. The Rutting Fucks
1841. Urgentlemen
1842. Telly Savales Lives!: Starring the Wax-Yet-Robot Players
1843. We Do All Our Laundry in the Sink
1844. The Obitu-Fairy
1845. Tactile Happenstance
1846. Carl's Bad
1847. Your Erection Will Last Longer Than Four Hours
1848. Jane! D'oh!
1849. A Remote Island of Clickers
1850. Udder Despair
1851. Do Re Mi So Horny
1852. The Confederate Dissertatin' Pickaninies
1853. We Also Have a Lawn Service
1854. 99.999% Larry
1855. Homogloben
1856. The "They've-Only-Been-Playing-10-Minutes?" Percussion Troupe
1857. Starsky and Cumberbatch
1858. I'maggedon Out
1859. The Constantly Applying Creams
1860. Ohhhh Myyyyy
1861. Al Gore Tries to Clap on Beat
1862. Only Hermaphrodites Are Allowed In Our Audience

1863. Sketchy Ethel
1864. Reptilium
1865. Everyone In This Band Has a Tennis Course
1866. Moonies at the Airport
1867. The Hotbreaths
1868. Everybody Maury Povich Tonight
1869. Twist and Ouch
1870. We've Placed a Magic Tuna Sandwich Under One of Your Seats!
1871. Hag Reflex
1872. The Mr. Ropers
1873. Sudoku: The Band
1874. Matt Class... Is My Name
1875. Calgon Leave Us Be
1876. The Smoke Monster from Lost Performs
1877. Radar O'Rhinoplasty
1878. Das Moot
1879. Roboy and Cygal Load Disks
1880. The Uncreative 1-Chord Verses
1881. We All Scream For Vanilla Ice
1882. Duct Tapin' the Warp Core
1883. Greg & Marcia's Sex Pact
1884. The BlasFems
1885. Leggo My Ego
1886. To Frack Or Not To That
1887. We Have No Sense of Humor Yet Feel Superior to All Comedy
1888. Frankenstein Pay With Paypal
1889. The Stomached
1890. Televised-Public-Trial Floor Sex

1891. Crack Needles & Cinnamon Stick
1892. Just Sounds
1893. Blow Job Honeycutt
1894. The Debit Or Credit Players
1895. Let's Muster!
1896. The Theatre Hoods
1897. Carpool Tunnel
1898. 10 10 Wins (Whatever That Is)
1899. L'il Fucky's First Damning
1900. The Band Who Can't Be Named Except For This Right Now
1901. Cap'n Chem-Berry
1902. Gene Rayburn: The Band
1903. Skunked Mammy
1904. Volume!: The Physical Meaning
1905. We Is Romantical And Like 'Dat
1906. Shakespeare's Desdemonial
1907. The Huge Ragu
1908. Who Let the Dorks Out
1909. Clingy Klingon
1910. Ten Times Me Is Me Again—Just Ask Me!
1911. American Idle
1912. Horg's Awesome Hex
1913. The Registered Sex Defenders
1914. Alottabad
1915. We Refuse To Take This Up a Minor 3rd
1916. Forbidden Line Dance
1917. Lenny Unrequited
1918. The Only Song You Know Comes First

1919. Dentures For All!
1920. "Marbled" Jorge and The Funyuns Construct
1921. Horizontalot
1922. The Updated Carts
1923. Overly Moral with The Obvious Inner Fears
1924. We Only Wear Merkin Wigs
1925. Exposo the Clown
1926. The Cankles
1927. Brian Boitano as Balki Bartakamuse Sings
1928. Go On, Git!
1929. Betty the Cracker
1930. Our Own Worst Enemy No. 1
1931. Please Stop Leaving Before the End
1932. Ringworm
1933. The Gropers
1934. "Desert" Strom and The Thurmond's
1935. Sporks & Skorts
1936. Everywhere We Perform There's a Burial Ground Underneath Us
1937. AvaBlanche!
1938. The Dung Beatles
1939. Try Opening Our CD - Am I Right?
1940. Please Return All the Picks
1941. Blaspheming Puppy
1942. When Mimes Attack
1943. The Cellophane-Encased Products
1944. Whorehouse Water Cracker (The WWC)
1945. Rabble Trouser

1946. Bubba Dumbo & The Loud-Truck Dorks
1947. Mallard
1948. The Haystack Needles
1949. Glengary GlenRossfromFriends
1950. Rappers Who Know the 3rd in G# Minor
1951. Botox For All!
1952. George Peppard Sings Although He's Dead
1953. Themz Wacky Rosecrutin' Eleven!
1954. We Snort Just For You
1955. Leprosy 'N Waffles
1956. The Gorton Fisherman Sings After Surgery
1957. Suck The Cock Fantastic
1958. Captain Gown
1959. The Afghanistan Girl From The Famous National Geographic Cover Lip-Syncs And Sex-Dances To Shitty Tunes But Gets Paid Handsomely And Moves Her Family To Malibu
1960. Vanilla Ice with The London Symphony
1961. Gut Rot
1962. The Fat Guy/Hot Chick Sitcoms
1963. Papt S'mores
1964. Girls, Let Us Be Your "Booby Trap"
1965. We Hate All Races Except Our Race: Now With Religion!
1966. Fuckernickle

1967. Boy-Band Troy and The Maybe-Gays
1968. The Pa-Rum-Pa-Pum-Pum's
1969. Irreverent Yocal
1970. The Boring Aspects Of Timbre
1971. We Kill Bugs Dead
1972. "Kissy" McLips and "Slippery" Ned
       Blast Off With Oily Discharge
1973. Taxidermy Live!
1974. Petered Peter
1975. The High Fructose Corn Syrup
       Dancers Sing
1976. Horton Hears a Show
1977. Hey You In The Back
1978. Tallyboybanana
1979. Everyone Gets A Saltine!
1980. Test Midget
1981. We Hate When Our Friends Do Well
1982. Toe Knee Handza
1983. OMG That Is So Like, Corrugated
1984. McGuilligoiter
1985. Crackie The Lobster Loves You
1986. Gotta Tell Ya'll: We're Registered
       Sex Offenders
1987. The Last Ensemble Cast On Earth
1988. Coocoocachewclock
1989. Our Love Is Stronger Than Glue
1990. Willie's On the Commode Again
1991. Creme De La Femmes
1992. Marcia Marcia Marcia Gay Hard On
1993. Only Codas!
1994. The Lying Rule Makers
1995. Bed, Bath and Bea Arthur

1996. Dude You Smell Like Garage
1997. What Else Will Hester Squat On?!
1998. Try Us, Punk
1999. We're Here To Stay—Again
2000. Sweet Home Alan Alda

by *David Forbes Brown*,
from the 4500 islands off Maine

Cover & back by **Scott A. Brown**

Photos by **Whittling Fog Photography**

The band set-ups on the cover and back are those of Maine's two premiere show bands, available for gigs:

The Jump City Jazz Band
&
The Jump City Social Club

The Jump City Jazz Band is the house band for Maine's only late night talk show—seen in the full state—**The Nite Show with Danny Cashman**. Special thanks to **Danny Cashman** for always championing this band name project, and for writing #287 in this book.

And finally, special thanks to my close friend **David Bramfitt**, who took time out of his busy day (composing music for television & film) to help me find errors.

I've written 6400+ band names, and these are my favorite. I had to leave many I love out of this, due to the whole "2000" thing.

I hope you enjoy them.

Yours truly,

Grizelda Thoates

Additional band names not provided by Scrabbleblatch Blubbitchplasty